John F. Kennedy

By Veda Boyd Jones

Subject Consultant
David G. Coleman, PhD
Assistant Professor, Miller Center of Public Affairs
University of Virginia, Charlottesville, Virginia

Reading Consultant
Cecilia Minden-Cupp, PhD
Former Director of the Language and Literacy Program
Harvard Graduate School of Education
Cambridge, Massachusetts

Children's Press®
A Division of Scholastic Inc.
New York Toronto London Auckland Sydney
Mexico City New Delhi Hong Kong
Danbury, Connecticut

Designer: Herman Adler Design
Photo Researcher: Caroline Anderson
The photo on the cover shows John F. Kennedy.

Library of Congress Cataloging-in-Publication Data

Jones, Veda Boyd.
  John F. Kennedy / by Veda Boyd Jones.
    p. cm. — (Rookie Biographies)
  Includes index.
  ISBN 0-516-25038-8 (lib. bdg.)   0-516-29797-X (pbk.)
  1. Kennedy, John F. (John Fitzgerald), 1917–1963—Juvenile literature.
  2. Presidents—United States—Biography—Juvenile literature. I. Title.
  II. Rookie biography.
  E842.Z9J66 2006
  973.922'092—dc22   2005021744

CHILDREN'S PRESS, and ROOKIE BIOGRAPHIES®, and associated
logos are trademarks and/or registered trademarks of Scholastic Library
Publishing. SCHOLASTIC and associated logos are trademarks and/or
registered trademarks of Scholastic Inc.
1 2 3 4 5 6 7 8 9 10 R 15 14 13 12 11 10 09 08 07 06

John F. Kennedy was the thirty-fifth president of the United States. Kennedy was born on May 29, 1917, in Massachusetts.

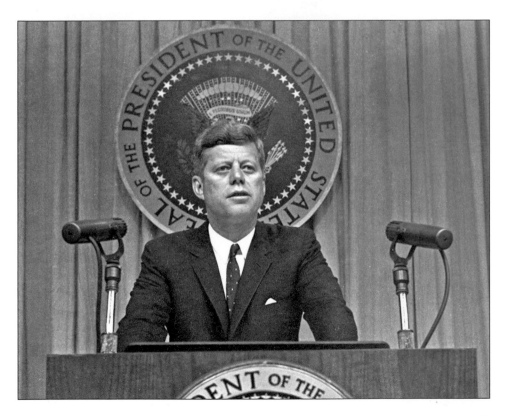

John F. Kennedy (right) and his older brother Joe in 1925

Kennedy had eight brothers and sisters. His parents wanted their children to be leaders.

Kennedy had one older brother, Joe. Kennedy's father hoped that someday Joe would be president of the United States.

Kennedy was often sick as a little boy. He missed a lot of school. But Kennedy was very smart and read books at home. He was able to learn many things this way.

Kennedy went to college when he got older. He also traveled to many countries.

Kennedy traveling during college

A naval battle in the Pacific during World War II

In 1941, Kennedy joined the U.S. Navy. The United States was fighting World War II against Germany, Italy, and Japan.

Kennedy was the leader of a patrol torpedo (PT) boat. PT boats were small, quick boats powered by a motor.

During one battle in the Pacific Ocean, a Japanese ship crashed into Kennedy's PT boat. The boat split in two.

Kennedy swam to a nearby island. He pulled another man to the island with him. Kennedy saved the man's life.

Kennedy in his naval uniform

Joe Kennedy Jr. during World War II

Kennedy's brother Joe Jr. was killed in World War II. Their father decided John should become president of the United States.

At age twenty-nine, Kennedy ran for office in the U.S. Congress. Congress makes laws for the United States.

Kennedy's big family helped him meet many voters. He won the election in 1946.

Kennedy speaking to voters in 1946

The Kennedys on their wedding day

Kennedy served in Congress
for fourteen years.

He married a woman named
Jacqueline Bouvier in 1953.
Many people called her Jackie.

Kennedy ran for president of the United States in 1960. He won and became the youngest man ever elected president. Kennedy was only forty-three years old.

Kennedy and his two children in the White House in 1962

Americans liked having Kennedy's young family in the White House. The country loved the president's two small children, Caroline and John Jr.

Kennedy and his wife went to Dallas, Texas, in 1963. They rode in a parade in a special car without a top. A man shot and killed President Kennedy while he was riding in the parade.

The president died on November 22, 1963. He was forty-six years old.

Kennedy's funeral in 1963

Kennedy greeting Peace Corps volunteers in 1962

Kennedy was president for almost three years. In that short time, he did many good things.

Kennedy started the Peace Corps. Americans in the Peace Corps go to other countries. They help people grow food and build schools.

Kennedy had many dreams for his country. He wanted people to travel to the Moon.

Kennedy also wanted peace with other countries in Europe. He met with European leaders to try to make this happen.

Kennedy meeting with foreign leader Nikita Khrushchev (right) during the early 1960s

Americans first landed on the Moon in 1969.

Today, the Peace Corps is still helping other countries. Americans have walked on the Moon. And the United States continues to work toward peace with all nations.

Words You Know

election

Jacqueline Bouvier Kennedy

Joe Kennedy Jr.

John F. Kennedy

30

Moon

White House

World War II

31

Index

About the Author

Veda Boyd Jones has written thirty-nine books. Her works include both fiction and nonfiction for adults and children. She lives with her husband in Missouri. They have three sons.

Photo Credits

Photographs © 2006: AP/Wide World Photos: 3, 23; Corbis Images: 7, 12, 30 bottom left (Bettmann), 8, 31 bottom right (Hulton-Deutsch Collection), 4, 15, 30 top left; John Fitzgerald Kennedy Library, Boston: 24 (Abbie Rowe/National Park Service), cover, 20, 31 bottom left (Cecil Stoughton/White House), 27 (U.S. Department of State Photograph), 11; NASA: 28, 31 top; The Image Works/Topham: 16, 19, 30 top right, 30 bottom right.

JAN 1 7 2007